FORD
MUSCLE CARS

Mike Mueller

MBI Publishing Company

First published in 1993 by MBI Publishing Company, 729 Prospect Avenue, PO Box 1, Osceola, WI 54020-0001 USA

MBI Publishing Company books are also available at discounts in bulk quantity for industrial or sales-promotional use. For details write to Special Sales Manager at Motorbooks International Wholesalers & Distributors, 729 Prospect Avenue, PO Box 1, Osceola, WI 54020-0001 USA.

Library of Congress Cataloging-in-Publication Data
Mueller, Mike.
    Ford muscle cars / Mike Mueller.
       p. cm. — (Enthusiast color series)
    Includes index.
    ISBN 0-87938-815-3
    1. Ford automobile—History. 2. Muscle cars—History. I. Title. II. Series.
TL215.F7M83   1993
629.222—dc20   93-13063

On the front cover: The 1965 Mustang fastback, the third body style introduced for Ford's original pony car. This example, owned by Paul and Carolyn LiCalsi, is equipped with a 289 and optional styled steel wheels. *Mike Mueller*

On the frontispiece: Ford's 289 Windsor small-block after the Shelby treatment. A quartet of Weber two-barrels orchestrate air and fuel delivery.

On the title page: Mustang's received a major face-lift in 1971, growing longer and wider. The Mach 1 pictured is powered by the optional 429 Cobra Jet.

On the back cover: The GT option turned the 1967 Fairlane into a muscular-looking boulevard cruiser. Eddie Kirkland owns this one.

Printed in Hong Kong

Contents

There Super Torque Ford engines climb hills like a homesick Swiss yodeler. One is available with 425 horsepower (a few more than the average private plane). Try <u>total performance</u> on your local Matterhorn.

—Ford advertisement, 1963

Acknowledgments

Special thanks go to all the men and women who allowed their performance Fords to be photographed for this book. In order of appearance, they are:

Charlie and Pam Plylar, Kissimmee, Florida: '71 429 Cobra Jet Mach 1 Mustang; Donald Farr, Lakeland, Florida: '66 Mustang GT; George Baumann, Davie, Florida: '67 Mercury Cougar XR-7 GT; Chris and Deborah Teeling, Enfield, Connecticut: '68-1/2 428 Cobra Jet Mustang; Carl Beck, Clearwater, Florida: '69 428 Cobra Jet Mercury Cougar Eliminator; Barry Larkins, Daytona Beach, Florida: '70 Boss 429 Mustang; Kurt and Connie Heber, Melbourne, Florida: '70 Boss 302 Mustang; Marc Troy, Jr., Latrobe, Pennsylvania: '64 Fairlane Thunderbolt (clone); Jerry and Carol Buczkowski, Mishawaka, Indiana: '66 427 Fairlane; Eddie Kirkland, Lakeland, Florida: '67 Fairlane GT; Jerry Sieradzki, South Bend, Indiana: '67 Mercury 427 Cyclone; Bob Kurtz, East Greenville, Pennsylvania: '69 Fairlane Cobra; Dan Andrews, Lakeland, Florida: '69 Talladega; Hubert and Sandi Miller, Melbourne, Florida: '60 Starliner; Luke and Sue Kirkland, Lakeland, Florida: '63 427 Galaxie; Bill and Barbara Jacobsen, Silver Dollar Classic Cars, Odessa, Florida: '64 427 Galaxie; Robert Schultz, Champaign, Illinois: '66 7-Litre convertible; Rick and Vicki Sattler, St. Petersburg, Florida: '67 7-Litre hardtop; Bill and Barbara Jacobsen, Silver Dollar Classic Cars, Odessa, Florida: '69 Galaxie XL GT 429 and '63 M-code Thunderbird Sports Roadster; Ed and Diann Kuziel, Tampa, Florida: '57 Thunderbird; Jeff Leggate, Savannah, Georgia: '65 Sunbeam Tiger; Dale Nichols, Orlando, Florida: 289 and 427 Cobras; Dave Robb, Titusville, Florida: '67 Shelby GT350 and '67 Shelby GT500.

Introduction

Total Performance

Ford's performance history actually began with a major step backwards. In February 1957, ultra-conservative general manager Robert McNamara agreed to an Automobile Manufacturers Association decree that Detroit's automakers cease all factory racing involvement, discontinue performance parts production, and refrain from using speed teasers in advertisements. Basically a clever ploy by General Motors head Harlow "Red" Curtice, the so-called AMA "ban" on factory performance left Ford Motor Company in the dust as Curtice's GM divisions continued competing in the horsepower race while McNamara focused his attentions on mundane pursuits, like the new, compact Falcon.

In November 1960, thirty-six year old Lee Iacocca stepped in as McNamara moved up. Recognizing that young, performance-minded buyers represented a growing force in the market, Iacocca reacted rapidly to reverse Ford's declining fortunes. Ford officials had already informed GM's front office in April 1959 of plans to offer performance options despite the AMA ban. The result was the 360hp 352ci Police Interceptor V-8, a powerplant that transformed the sleek '60 Starliner coupe into what may best be described as Ford's first muscle car. Progenitor of a long line of hot, big-block, FE-series V-8s, Ford's 352 Police Interceptor was followed by a

Opposite page
Not all Ford muscle cars wore galloping horses or striking cobras. The R-code 425hp 427-equipped Fairlane (left) and W-code 410hp 427 Cyclone (right) were built on intermediate-sized chassis with an eye cast toward drag strip and NASCAR competition. From 1963–67, Ford offered both versions of the 427—the R-code featuring twin four-barrels, the W-code using one four-barrel—although the '66 427 Fairlane used only the twin-carb variety. When four hood pins are pulled, the 427 Fairlane's fiberglass hood simply lifts off.

procession of bigger and better power sources with displacements growing to 390ci in 1961, 406ci in 1962, 427ci in 1963, and 428ci in 1966.

In June 1962, Henry Ford II officially announced his company would no longer comply with the 1957 AMA edict, claiming that "We feel we can better establish our own standards of conduct with respect to the manner in which the performance of our vehicles is to be promoted and advertised." The following April, Iacocca introduced his "Total Performance" campaign. "We at Ford believe in performance," he told the press, "because the search for performance—Total Performance—made the automobile the wonderfully efficient, pleasurable machine it is today—and will make it better tomorrow." And with that, the race was on.

In 1963 and 1964, full-sized Fords powered by the famed 427ci FE V-8 were both boulevard brutes and racing champions. Then came the mass-market miracle called Mustang. Introduced in April 1964, Iacocca's baby created a new breed aptly named "pony car." Originally offering only small-block power, with the 271hp High-Performance 289 representing the top performance option, the Mustang was redesigned for 1967 to make room for the big-block FEs. And in April 1968, the 335hp 428ci Cobra Jet V-8 transformed Ford's pony cars into true street killers.

The next year, Ford made the 428 Cobra Jet standard in a mid-sized body, creating the Fairlane Cobra, a no-nonsense performance machine intended to compete with Plymouth's Road Runner. On the flip side of the coin, 1969 also marked the introduction of the stylish Mach 1 Mustang, a car that offered every bit as much pizzazz as performance. And at the head of the pony car herd were three racing-inspired models: the Trans Am-tested Boss 302; its Mercury cousin, the Cougar Eliminator; and the big-block brute Boss 429 Mustang.

For 1970, Ford debuted a new big-block, the 385-series 429ci Thunder Jet, an engine that offered Torino Cobra buyers 360hp as standard equipment. Like its 428ci counterpart in the Mustang ranks, the '70 Torino Cobra's 429 could also be equipped with Cobra Jet equipment, upping the power ante to 375hp. Returning for a farewell appearance in 1971, the 429 Cobra Jet represented Ford's last great muscle car powerplant as the curtain came down on Dearborn performance. By 1972, strict emissions standards and hefty insurance costs spelled the end for the big-block Cobra Jets, leaving the small-block 351 Cleveland V-8 to carry the Blue Oval banner into the seventies. And when Iacocca replaced the third-generation Mustang with the little Mustang II in 1974, it was made painfully clear that a new age had dawned.

First appearing on full-sized fenders early in 1963, this emblem represented Ford Motor Company's hottest underhood offering until the famed 428 Cobra Jet emerged early in 1968. In 1966, the 427ci FE-series big-block V-8 made its debut in intermediate ranks within Fairlane sheet metal, followed by Mercury's 427 Cyclone in '67. The 427 was last offered in detuned, single-carb, 390hp form in 1968. Few were sold, and the majority of those were included as part of Mercury's GT-E Cougar package.

Chapter 1

Wild Horses

Ford's Mustang Kicked off a New Breed

On April 17, 1964, Ford Motor Company unleashed a sales blitz the likes of which Detroit had never seen, rushing the Mustang to market after first teasing the press with a small, two-seat sports car prototype in 1962. Commonly credited in full to Lee Iacocca, Ford's phenomenal pony car was instant front-page news, making simultaneous appearances on the covers of both *Time* and *Newsweek*. Dealers were swamped with orders for the affordable sportster with the long hood, bucket seats, and floor shifter. Within twelve months, the Mustang had broken Ford's own record for first-year sales established by the utilitarian Falcon in 1960. After twenty-four months, total pony car production had surpassed one million.

For most buyers, Ford's Mustang offered economical, practical transportation with a sporty flair. Standard power originally came from a feeble 170ci six-cylinder, with optional 260ci and 289ci Windsor V-8s waiting in the wings. Anxious to harness the new pony car performance image, Ford engineers introduced the truly hot 271hp "K-code" High-Performance 289 in June 1964. Following in August was a sporty "2+2" fastback body style joining the hardtop and convertible models. Then in April 1965, Ford debuted the GT equipment group to help mark the Mustang's one-year anniversary. Featuring various suspension upgrades and appearance items, the GT package represented the top of the heap in pony car performance for 1965 and '66.

Opposite page
What a difference five years can make. In 1966, Ford's first-generation Mustang (right) was a relatively nimble, sporty compact armed only with a Windsor small-block in top performance trim. By 1971, the third-generation Mustang had grown into anything but a compact and could be ordered with Dearborn's largest, most powerful V-8, the 429 Cobra Jet, rated at 370hp.

GT exterior features included fog lamps and a special grille bar, twin exhaust trumpets exiting through the rear valance panel, a lower body stripe, "GT" fender identification, and these optional knock-off wheel covers. Attractive, 14in, styled steel wheels were also available.

But then came the competition's response. GM debuted its own pony cars in 1967, Chevrolet's Camaro and Pontiac's Firebird, both featuring optional big-block V-8s. Also new for '67 was Mercury's Cougar, a longer, more luxurious version of its Mustang cousin. To stay in the race, Ford Motor Company offered the venerable 390ci FE-series big-block V-8 as an option for both the Cougar and Mustang, a move that required enlarging the '67 Mustang body, an idea with which Iacocca wholeheartedly disagreed. Even with big-block power, however, Dearborn's pony cars were quickly left behind by high-powered rivals, a situation that was rectified with a vengeance the following year.

In April 1968, Ford introduced the 428 Cobra Jet Mustang, a super-stock drag car for the street that *Hot Rod*'s Eric Dahlquist called "the fastest regular production sedan ever built." On the street, the new Cobra Jet Mustangs were easy 14sec performers; at the track, they were NHRA Winternational champions—either way, Ford had a real winner.

Complementing the Cobra Jet's optional 335hp in 1969 was the new Mach 1 Sports-Roof Mustang offering loads of sporty looks, some nice luxury touches, and ample beef underneath. New as well for '69 were the Boss 302 and Boss 429 Mustangs, the former built to homologate a hot, small-block pony car for Trans Am competition, the latter doing the same for its NASCAR-inspired engine only. Mercury's Cougar Eliminator was also introduced in '69 with Trans Am competition in mind, although it was available with a full range of optional FoMoCo power sources ranging from the high-winding Boss 302 small-block to the stump-pulling 428 Cobra Jet big-block.

The 428 CJ returned for one last year as a Mustang option in 1970. Meanwhile, the 351 Cleveland small-block was debuting as the Boss 429 was being phased out. Featuring free-breathing, Boss 302-type canted-valve heads, the hot 300hp 351 Cleveland was offered as standard equipment under '70 Cougar Eliminator hoods. Both the Eliminator and Boss 302 Mustang would follow the Boss 429 by year's end.

Big news for 1971 was a radically larger Mustang body and an optional 429ci 385-

To celebrate the Mustang's first birthday, Ford introduced two attractive options packages in April 1965: the interior decor group—often called the "pony interior" for its "running horses" seat inserts—and the GT equipment group. Available only with 289ci four-barrel V-8s, the 225hp version or the 271hp "Hi Po," the GT option group included various appearance pieces along with some serious performance hardware. Front disc brakes were included, as was a special handling package that featured heavier springs, stiffer shocks, quicker 22:1 steering, and a larger front stabilizer bar. Inside, a five-dial instrument cluster was added.

Mercury's Cougar debuted in 1967 on a stretched Mustang platform with simulated leather buckets, hideaway headlights, and V-8 power all as standard equipment. Amply impressed, *Motor Trend's* editors named it their "Car of the Year." Like Ford's Mustang, Mercury's top performance Cougar featured the GT package, a $323 option that included power front discs, a performance handling package, Firestone Wide Oval rubber, and the 320hp 390ci big-block V-8. According to *Car and Driver*, a '67 Cougar GT could run 0–60mph in 6.5sec. This GT is also an XR-7 model, a fully loaded Cougar option package introduced in February 1967. XR-7 features included a wood-rimmed steering wheel, black-face competition-type instrumentation in a simulated walnut dash, toggle switches, an overhead console, a leather-covered T-handle automatic transmission shifter, and combination leather/vinyl seats.

series V-8 in place of the 428 CJ. Available with or without ram air, and in Cobra Jet and Super Cobra Jet form, the 429 CJ was rated at 370hp regardless of accompanying equipment. And with the Boss 302 and Boss 429 gone, Ford rolled out its Boss 351 Mustang for '71, perhaps as a farewell to pony car performance. Powered by a High Output 300hp 351 Cleveland, the Boss 351 was a high-13sec screamer, as well as a suitable send-off for the Mustang performance bloodline. Once the big 429s were gone after '71, only the Cleveland small-blocks were around to carry on, and that legacy ended as well with the Mustang II's arrival in 1974.

Having fallen behind the pony car performance crowd, Ford made an impressive comeback in 1968, introducing the 428 Cobra Jet Mustang on April 1. Available as fastbacks, hardtops, or convertibles, all Cobra Jet Mustangs were GT models, meaning they were equipped with heavy-duty suspension, styled steel wheels wearing F70 rubber, fog lamps, body side C-stripes, "GT" fender emblems, and quad exhaust tips. Additional standard Cobra Jet Mustang features included a functional Ram-Air hood with distinctive black striping, front disc brakes, and a heavy-duty 9in rearend.

This '68-1/2 Cobra Jet Mustang still wears its Tasca Ford dealer emblem. Tasca Ford, located in East Providence, Rhode Island, was a mecca for Ford performance fans in the sixties, and it was Bob Tasca who actually inspired Ford to build the Cobra Jet Mustang. Not satisfied with the 390ci-equipped Mustang, Tasca's men built their own "King of the Road" prototype in 1967 using various FE-series V-8 components. Tasca then demonstrated his KR Mustang in Dearborn, leading to Ford's decision to build the 428 Cobra Jet.

Left
Inside, four-speed Cobra Jet Mustangs were equipped with an 8000rpm tach as standard; tachs were optional when the C6 automatic transmission was chosen. Four-speed Cobra Jets also received staggered rear shocks, while all 428 CJ Mustangs came with braced shock towers up front. Bottom line was about $3,600, roughly $1,000 more than a base 2+2 '68 Mustang. According to *Hot Rod*, a specially prepared Cobra Jet Mustang prototype roared through the quarter-mile in 13.56sec at 106.64mph. Actual quarter-mile performance for a typical Cobra Jet was probably in the low 14sec range.

Ford engineers based the Cobra Jet V-8 on a 428ci passenger car block. On top went 427 low-riser heads, a cast-iron copy of the aluminum Police Interceptor intake manifold, and a 735cfm Holley four-barrel carburetor.

A 390 GT cam, PI connecting rods, and 10.6:1 pistons completed the package. Advertised output was 335hp, a conservative figure that fooled very few.

Mercury's Cougar Eliminator first appeared in prototype form at the Los Angeles Auto Show in October 1968. The model created enough of a stir to justify regular production, and the official introduction came in April 1969. Everything about the car was eye-popping, from its radiant paint schemes and large hood scoop, to its front and rear spoilers. Competition suspension, including heavy springs and shocks and a large front sway bar, was standard, with a rear sway bar optionally available.

Eliminator color choices numbered five—blue, orange, yellow, gold, and green—all of them glaring. External identification on 1969 models included a bodyside stripe that terminated in "Eliminator" lettering just behind the door; for '70, the stripe ran the length of the car and the lettering was moved to the lower rear quarters. Production of Eliminators in '69 was 2,411 and 2,200 in 1970.

Standard Eliminator power in 1969 came from a 290hp 351 Windsor small-block V-8. Available at extra cost was a 320hp 390ci FE, the 290hp Boss 302 canted-valve small-block, and this 335hp 428 Cobra Jet big-block. In a *Super Stock & Drag Illustrated* magazine test, a '69 428 CJ Cougar ran the quarter-mile in 13.91sec, topping out at 103.9mph.

Standard Eliminator equipment included F70x14in Goodyear Polyglas rubber on styled steel wheels with blank center caps. Eliminators equipped with the optional 428 Cobra Jet V-8, like this one, also received higher rate springs, an even thicker front sway bar, and staggered rear shocks.

The Cobra Jet will be the utter delight of every Ford lover and the bane of all the rest because, quite frankly, it is the fastest running Pure Stock in the history of man.

—*Hot Rod*, March 1968

Previous pages
Ford built the legendary Boss 429 Mustang to homologate the big Boss 429 V-8 for NASCAR competition under mid-sized model hoods. Under NASCAR rules, a stock engine was legal as long as it was installed in at least 500 models sold to the public. Since the specific model used wasn't important, Dearborn officials decided to install the Boss 429 in pony car sheet metal. Partially assembled '69 and '70 Mustang SportsRoofs were sent to the Kar Kraft works in Brighton, Michigan, where all Boss 429 modifications were made. A front chin spoiler and large, functional hood scoop were standard on the Boss 429. Hood scoops on '69 models were painted body color, while '70 Boss 429s used a black scoop.

Modifications required to fit the Boss 429 into the Mustang's engine bay included moving the spring towers one inch farther apart. To help compensate for the new nose-heavy stance, the front A-arms were also lowered one inch. Among chassis features were front disc brakes, Gabriel shocks, and a rear stabilizer bar. Boss 429 Mustangs also received fender decal identification, dual color-keyed racing mirrors, and 15in Magnum 500 wheels. An engine oil cooler under the hood and a trunk-mounted battery were part of the package as well.

Featuring aluminum "semi-hemi" heads with staggered valves, Ford's Boss 429 V-8 could breathe with the best of them—so well, in fact, that the standard 735cfm Holley four-barrel couldn't keep up with the big engine's appetite. Advertised output was 375hp and 450lb-ft of torque. While the first 279 '69 Boss 429s had magnesium valve covers, remaining '69s and all '70s wore these aluminum covers. Known as

NASCAR versions, the first 279 Boss 429 engines used hydraulic cams and 1/2in connecting rod bolts and can be identified by their "820 S" engine tag code. The other 580 '69 models and most '70 Boss 429s received the 820 T engine with a mechanical cam and 3/8in rod bolts. Extremely rare is the 820 A Boss 429 which featured minor modifications to the Thermactor smog equipment.

KK 429 NASCAR 2206

All Boss 429 Mustangs received this Kar Kraft production number sticker on the driver's door denoting the cars' status as NASCAR homologation models. Production of Boss 429s in Brighton spanned but twelve months beginning in January 1969, with '70 models first rolling down the line that September. KK production numbers for 1969 Boss 429s ran from 1201 to 2059 as total production reached 859. This Grabber Blue '70 Boss 429 is one of 499 built; accordingly, '70 model KK numbers ran from 2060 to 2558

Right
Lowering the Boss 429, widening its track, and using big F60 Goodyear rubber on 15in Magnum 500 wheels required some custom modification to the front fender wheel openings to allow clearance. Kar Kraft's people obtained ample clearance by rolling in the wheel opening lip.

Ford president Semon "Bunkie" Knudsen, a performance-minded manager with a background in GM projects like the Z/28 Camaro, simply demanded that Ford build "absolutely the best-handling street car available on the American market." The result was the Boss 302 Mustang, first offered in 1969, and again in '70. Chassis engineer Matt Donner met Knudsen's demand with fat F60 rubber on 15in wheels, competition springs, a stiff front sway bar, and staggered heavy-duty shocks in back. After driving a '69 Boss 302, *Car and Driver*'s staff called it "the best handling Ford ever to come out of Dearborn and [it] just may be the new standard by which everything from Detroit must be judged." Designer Larry Shinoda, a former GM employee probably best known for his work on the '63 Corvette Sting Ray, supplied the Boss 302's exterior appeal with graphics, spoilers, and slats. A front chin spoiler, black-striped hood, "Boss 302" bodyside stripes that draped over the cowl, dual color-keyed racing mirrors, and blacked-out rear deck and cove panel were all standard. Optional dress-up items included rear window slats and a rear deck wing. Thanks to the big 15in, 60-series tires, Boss 302s had their front fender lips rolled in similar fashion to Boss 429 front fenders. Magnum 500 wheels were optional.

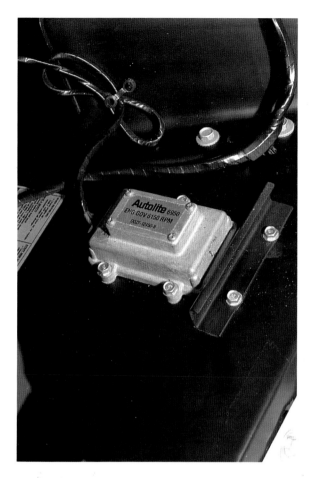

Left
With free-breathing, canted-valve Cleveland heads equipped with big valves (2.23in intake, 1.71in exhaust), the Boss 302 could wind like nobody's business, up to 7000rpm by factory claims, which is why a rev limiter was included in the package. A 780cfm Holley carburetor on an aluminum intake delivered fuel/air to the combustion chambers with the help of a .477in lift, 290-degree duration solid-lifter cam. Compression was 10.5:1. In 1970, intake valve size decreased to 2.19in and chrome valve covers were replaced by aluminum units. Maximum output for the Boss 302 was advertised as 290hp at 5800rpm.

Above left
All Boss 302 Mustangs in 1969 and '70 came equipped with this Autolite rev limiter mounted on the engine compartment wall just ahead of the driver's side shock tower. If not disconnected or removed by the owner—a common occurrence—this limiter restricted the high-winding Boss small-block to 6150rpm.

A total restyle in 1971 transformed the Mustang into "a fat pig" in Iacocca's terms, but a bigger body built around Ford's biggest engines was what Bunkie Knudsen had wanted during his short Dearborn tenure. In keeping with tradition, the '71 Mach 1 featured a host of performance imagery and heavy-duty hardware. A black honeycomb grille with rectangular "sportslamps," color-keyed urethane front bumper, dual racing mirrors, black or argent (depending on exterior color) lower body paint, special body side stripe, blacked out rear cove, chrome exhaust extensions, and appropriate "Mach1 Mustang" fender and rear deck decals were all standard. Optional dress-up included a front chin spoiler, Magnum 500 wheels, and rear wing spoiler. Standard 14in wheels featured flat hubcaps and trim rings. Although complaints about its girth and poor rearward visibility were many, most felt the '71 Mach 1 was an attractive machine. As *Sports Car Graphic* explained, "whatever [the car] isn't, it is exciting, and . . . no Mach 1 is going to rust in a showroom."

Left

Standard power for the '71 Mach 1 was a 302ci two-barrel small-block, but if real muscle was the aim, the only choice was the optional 429 Cobra Jet, available with an optional ram air hood and/or the Drag Pack equipment which then transformed it into a Super Cobra Jet. Beefier internals, an external oil cooler, and a choice between a 3.91:1 Traction-Lok or 4.30:1 Detroit Locker rearend were just a few of the Super Cobra Jet's features. With or without ram air, Cobra Jet or Super Cobra Jet, the performance 429s were advertised by Ford at 370hp in 1971. At the track, that power translated into a 13.97sec 100mph quarter-mile run according to *Super Stock* magazine.

The blacked-out treatment and tie-down pins were standard Mach 1 fare in 1971, but the NACA-ducted hood was an option with the base 302ci small-block. Although ordering a 351 or 429 automatically included the NACA hood, the twin scoops weren't functional unless the optional ram air equipment was ordered as well.

Chapter 2

Mid-Sized Maulers

Thunderbolts, Cyclones, and Cobras

Named after Henry Ford's estate, Ford's Fairlane nameplate first appeared on Dearborn's flagships in 1955. Replaced at the top by the Galaxie lineup in 1959, the Fairlane moniker was last used in the full-sized ranks in 1961, but reappeared the following year. "Some cars have new names," read factory brochures, "this name has a new car." Introduced for 1962, the new intermediate Fairlane was nearly one foot shorter than the big Galaxie, yet was eight inches longer than the compact Falcon. Also introduced that year was an innovative, lightweight V-8 created through a technique known as thin-wall casting. Initially displacing 221ci, the Fairlane V-8 was 90lb lighter and considerably more compact than the popular Chevrolet small-block V-8.

Early performance enhancements included the mid-year 1962 "Lively Ones" promotion, when Ford Motor Company rolled out the Fairlane 500 Sports Coupe. Included in the Sports Coupe deal were bucket seats and a mini-console. Also available at extra cost was the 260 Challenger V-8, a bored-out version of the 221. In 1963, engineers again punched out displacement mid-year, resulting in the 289 Challenger V-8, a reasonably hot small-block that delivered 271hp in optional "High-Performance" trim.

Big news in 1964 involved two new offerings, one for the street and one for the

Opposite page
Introduced in the spring of 1966 as yet another ploy to legalize a high-performance package for super-stock drag racing, Ford's second 427 Fairlane wasn't quite as radical as the '64 Thunderbolt, yet was a still a force to be reckoned with. Built as no-nonsense racing machines, all were Wimbledon White Fairlane 500 hardtops (no XLs or GTs) armed with the 425hp, dual-carb 427ci medium-riser V-8. Standard equipment included front disc brakes and a fiberglass scooped hood held down by pins at all four corners.

Homologating a specific performance model for NHRA super-stock drag racing in 1964 required a production run of at least fifty units; Ford ended up building twice that many Thunderbolts, which ran as A/FX (factory experimental) competitors until the first fifty were completed. To save weight, these racing Fairlanes were equipped with various fiberglass components, including the distinctive teardrop-scooped hood (required to clear the 427 High Riser's dual carburetors), fenders, and front bumpers (some later Thunderbolts wore aluminum bumpers). Screens took the place of the two inside headlights as those openings were used to feed cooler, denser air directly to the carbs via two huge ducts. A Detroit Locker rearend containing 4.56:1 gears and held in place by welded-on traction bars brought up the rear. This '64 Fairlane street machine was built by its owner to Thunderbolt specs and features a modern pro-street narrowed rearend and aftermarket wheels and tires.

track. For the street, Mercury unleashed its Cyclone on mid-sized Comet buyers. Using the "Hi-Po" 289 as its top optional power source, the Comet Cyclone also featured some nice performance-look items, including buckets and a console, a three-spoke sport steering wheel, a dash-mounted tach, and simulated chrome-wheel hubcaps. At the same time, Ford was making a name for itself among the factory super-stock crowd with its Thunderbolt, an 11sec, 427ci-powered lightweight Fairlane that helped Dearborn win 1964's NHRA Manufacturers Cup. Thunderbolts did a lot for Ford's image at the track, but they couldn't make up for the fact that Fairlanes were rapidly falling behind in the race on Main Street USA.

In 1966, Fairlanes and Comets received all-new sheet metal, as well as big-block power and a sporty GT package. Standard with the GT and GTA (A for automatic) Fairlanes and Cyclones was the 335hp 390ci FE-series V-8. Bucket seats, heavy-duty suspension, and various dress-up tricks were also included. Not available with the GT equipment, but shoehorned into more than fifty '66 Fairlanes was Ford's legendary 425hp 427ci V-8. Created to make the model legal for super-stock drag racing, the 427 Fairlane appeared again in 1967, joined by equally mighty 427 Comets.

Ford finally made a major impression on the average performance-minded Joe on the street with an affordable mid-sized muscle machine in 1969, rolling out the Fairlane Cobra in fastback and formal-roof form. Mar-

With a standard oval 427 air cleaner in place of the Thunderbolt air box and twin ducts, the 427 High Riser's tall manifold and twin 720cfm Holley four-barrels can be seen. High Riser cylinder heads featured large, "tall" ports, and creating a matching High Riser intake allowed fuel/air mixture a more direct path from the carbs to the combustion chambers. But it also made hood clearance impossible, thus the reason for the trademark teardrop hood. Fitting the 427 into the Fairlane's engine bay required cutting down the shock towers, which were then reinforced with welded steel plates.

keted as a budget-conscious super car along the lines of Plymouth's Road Runner, the Cobra featured few frills, but was powered by a standard 335hp courtesy of the 428 Cobra Jet V-8. In 1970, the Cobra became an upscale Torino model and traded its 428 CJ for the new 429 Thunder Jet. Armed with the optional 375hp 429 Super Cobra Jet, the '70

Cobra ranked as one of Ford's all-time hottest offerings, running the quarter in 13.63sec according to *Super Stock* magazine. Although the optional 429 Cobra Jet was still around in 1971, standard Torino Cobra power came from a 351 Cleveland small-block, an able performer but an imposter in the minds of big-block buyers.

By 1972, Detroit's mid-sized muscle game was all but over, with Ford's Cleveland-powered Gran Torino serving only to preserve powerful memories for a few more years.

Left
Additional weight was trimmed from a Thunderbolt by deleting insulation and sound deadener. Lightweight buckets and a rubber floor mat did away with a few pounds as well. Plexiglass replaced side and rear glass, and the rear quarter window winding mechanisms were deleted. Thunderbolts were equipped with either four-speeds or Lincoln automatic transmissions.

Right
Production of '66 427 Fairlanes—identified externally only by two small fender emblems—totalled but fifty-seven cars. For 1967, Ford extended the 427 option into the top-line XL ranks (GTs were still not available) and a few automatic-equipped 427 Fairlanes were also included among the 163 '67models built. Standard in 1966, the lift-off fiberglass hood with its functional scoop became a 427 Fairlane option in 1967.

With performance being the main intention, all '66 427 Fairlanes were Plain Jane machines throughout, as this bench seat interior attests. All were four-speed cars (automatics weren't available) and all had their heaters and radios deleted.

Right
Buyers interested in equipping a FoMoCo intermediate with 427 power in 1967 were actually presented with a choice or two, a situation contrary to the '66 427 Fairlane which basically presented a take-it-or-leave-it proposition. White was no longer the only color, and Mercury customers were also invited to the party as the 427 made its way into '67 Mercs ranging from the low-priced Comet 202 all the way up to the top-dog Cyclone. According to Ford Motor Company records, only eight '67 Cyclones were produced using R-code and W-code 427s.

Left
Choosing the 410hp 427 added about $900
to a Cyclone sticker in 1967 (the 425hp 427 cost
nearly $1,130). Along with the big FE-series V-8,
additional race-ready equipment included front
disc brakes, an 11.5in heavy-duty clutch, a
top-loader four-speed, and a nodular 9in rearend
containing beefy thirty-one-spline axles and
3.89:1 gears. Extra cooling was supplied by a
larger radiator with a clutch fan, and a 42-amp
alternator and heavy-duty battery were
also included.

Being an upscale Cyclone, this '67 427
Mercury offers a bit more pizzazz inside in
comparison to the more mundane '66 427
Fairlane. Standard Cyclone features included
bucket seats and a simulated wood-rimmed
steering wheel. This Jamaican Yellow 427
Cyclone even has a radio and a clock.

In standard form, the '69 Fairlane Cobra was indeed an "economy supercar," as the press called it nearly twenty-five years ago. Base price for the rarely seen formal roof variety was $3,206, making it one of the best bangs for the buck in its day (the more popular fastback was even cheaper at $3,183). Armed with a 335hp 428 Cobra Jet V-8 backed by a four-speed, the Fairlane Cobra was an easy mid-14sec stoplight warrior. Adding the optional Ram-Air equipment, which made the Cobra's hood scoop functional, lowered ETs into the low 14sec range. Hood pins and a black-out grille were also included in the deal.

Preceding pages
Introduced in 1966 with standard big-block power, the Fairlane GT took a step backward in 1967 as the 335hp 390ci V-8 was exchanged for the 289 Challenger V-8 small-block. Top power option in '67 was the 320hp 390. GT features included power front disc brakes, a black-out grille, "GT" identification, bucket seats, and a sporty "power dome" hood. The attractive styled steel wheels were optional. Adding the optional Selectshift Cruise-O-Matic C6 automatic transmission transformed a Fairlane GT into a GTA. Total production for '67 GT and GTA hardtops was 18,670; convertibles numbered 2,117.

Fairlane Cobra buyers had but one choice under the hood, but no one was complaining. Heart of this snake was Ford's famed 428 Cobra Jet, conservatively rated at 335hp. Maximum torque was 445lb-ft at 3400rpm with 10.7:1 compression. The large rubber "doughnut" sealed the air cleaner to the hood's underside as part of the optional Ram-Air package. Ram-Air didn't change advertised output, but the improvement was easily recorded by the seat of your pants.

The Fairlane Cobra's staggered rear shocks helped the leaf spring rear suspension stay tight during hard launches. Early Fairlane Cobras apparently carried large Cobra decals, but most models you'll see wear small cast Cobra emblems on each front fender and the deck lid. Options on this Black Jade '69 Cobra include the vinyl roof, chrome styled steel wheels, power front disc brakes, and power steering. For 1970 and '71, Cobras were based on Ford's top-line intermediate, the Torino.

Aerodynamic in 1967 meant all the vertical surfaces were angled as though bent by the wind.

—Randy Leffingwell,
American Muscle

A four-speed stick was standard Fairlane Cobra equipment in 1969, but practically everything else you see was optional, including the sport steering wheel, bucket seats and console, AM/FM stereo, and 6000rpm tach.

Other than its blacked-out hood and contrasting upper body stripe (not visible in this photo), a '69 Talladega received no other special exterior cosmetic identification save for "T" badges above the door handles and another large "T" on the dummy gas cap in back. NASCAR-inspired tricks also included special rocker panels that were rolled up one inch (at great expense) to create a higher measuring point for inspection officials, meaning track-ready Talladega bodies could be lowered and still stay within legal limits.

Following pages
Built with NASCAR superspeedways in mind, Ford's '69 Talladega may have looked a bit odd with its extended snout, but guffaws quickly faded once this aerodynamic beast hit the track. NASCAR rules required Detroit's automakers to build at least 500 street-going examples of any given bodystyle to make that bodystyle legal for competition. Ford ended up building 745 Talladegas. A flush grille, a modified Fairlane rear bumper, and fender extensions accompanied by a sloping header panel transformed the '69 Talladega's frontend into a wind-cheating airfoil. Mercury tried the same tactic in 1969 with its Cyclone Spoiler II.

Although actual NASCAR racing versions of the Talladega were powered by the Boss 429 powerplant—itself homologated for competition as a Mustang model option—streetside versions were all equipped with 335hp 428 Cobra Jet V-8s backed by C6 automatics. Although brochures mentioned optional Ram-Air, it is believed only two prototypes were built with a functional hood scoop. Talladegas also featured a nodular 9in rear with 3.25:1 gears and thirty-one-spline axles. Included as well were staggered rear shocks, features that came standard on four-speed Cobra Jet Fords

Extending the Talladega's nose required a mini-maze of braces and supports in front of the radiator bulkhead. Hanging out about five inches beyond stock Fairlane specs, the Talladega's front bumper was a Fairlane rear unit cut up and rewelded in a "V" configuration.

Chapter 3

Big Cubes In Big Cars

Fast Full-Sized Fords

While Dearborn was abiding by the 1957 AMA ruling limiting factory performance, GM divisions in the late fifties were busy behind the scenes developing quite an array of hot hardware—the prowess of which was demonstrated by multiple high-profile victories on NASCAR tracks. But just when it seemed Pontiac and Chevrolet would run away and hide, Ford put itself back in the race.

On April 27, 1959, Dearborn officials both informed their GM counterparts of a plan to market high-performance options and suggested everyone take a second look at the AMA agreement. Meanwhile, a three-man team working under the guise of "law enforcement parts development" had set out to put Ford back on the performance track. Included were engineers Dave Evans, Don Sullivan, and John Cowley. The fruit of their labor was Ford's first factory-delivered muscle car powerplant, the 352 Interceptor Special V-8, an FE-series big-block displacing 352ci. Priced at $125, the optional Interceptor Special featured a hot solid-lifter cam, 10.6:1 compression, a dual-point distributor, and an aluminum four-barrel intake. Advertised output was 360hp.

In 1961, the 352 was bored and stroked out to 390ci and maximum horsepower jumped to 375. Later in the year, an optional triple-carb setup was made available over dealer parts counters, as was Ford's first floor-

Opposite page
Ford's last full-sized performance model was the Galaxie XL GT, offered in 1968 and '69. Originally priced at $204.64, the GT equipment group included heavy-duty suspension, power front discs, low-restriction dual exhausts, wide-oval rubber, mag-type wheel covers, GT emblems, and special body side "C-stripes." A 390ci FE-series big-block V-8 was the XL GT's standard power source, but this '69 model is equipped with the optional 429ci 385-series big-block.

Long, low, and wide, Ford's all-new flagship for 1960 was the Starliner coupe, a boulevard cruiser that actually measured 1.5-inches wider than federal highway standards allowed. Equipped with the optional 360hp 352 Interceptor Special V-8, a '60 Starliner basically became Dearborn's first muscle car. At Ford's Romeo, Michigan test track, a 360hp prototype managed 152.6mph, leading *Hot Rod*'s Ray Brock to conclude that though " . . . it took several years, we think Ford has the right answer for 1960."

shifted four-speed transmission. When topped by the three Holley two-barrels, the 390's output was listed at 401hp.

Both the four-on-the-floor and the triple carbs became regular factory options in 1962. Also new for '62 was the 406ci FE big-block, yet another bore-job introduced in December 1961. More ruggedly constructed throughout, the 406 was offered in two forms, a 385hp version with a single four-barrel and the 405hp beast with the triple Holleys. Immediately after the 406 debuted, Ford announced the XL trim package to showcase its hot performance powerplants. Including various exterior dress-up pieces and a sporty bucket seat interior, the Galaxie XL instantly became Ford's flagship. Mercury also made the same mid-year move, rolling out its S-55 Monterey.

The Total Performance campaign kicked into high gear in 1963 as Dearborn designers introduced aerodynamics to their full-sized lineup. Yet another mid-year move attached a sweeping "fastback" to the Galaxie body, making it far more formidable on NASCAR super-speedways. And to help move that big body, engineers beefed up the FE block one more time, resulting in the famed 427. Offered in basically the same form from early 1963 through 1966, the 427 pumped out 425hp with dual four-barrel carbs, or 410hp when fed by a single Holley four-barrel. Appearing briefly for the last time in 1968, a detuned 427 was rated at 390hp.

Kings of NASCAR in 1963 and 1964, the 427 Galaxie's thunder began to fade once intermediate muscle cars hit the scene led by

On December 15, 1961, Ford announced a bigger and better FE-series big-block, the 406. Increasing the 390's bore in a recast, beefed-up block produced the 406, which was offered with one four-barrel carburetor or three Holley two-barrels. Output was 385hp and 405hp, respectively. Compression went as high as 11.4:1. The list of bright dress-up items for the top performance 406s was extensive, including the valve covers, master cylinder cap, fan shroud, radiator cap, dipstick, oil filler cap, and fuel filter.

Pontiac's GTO. Although still available from 1965 through 1967, full-sized 427s were rarely seen. In a move to renew interest in powerful big cars, Ford introduced its 7-Litre Galaxie in 1966, a model offering more pizzazz than actual performance. Standard 7-Litre power came from a 345hp 428ci big-block V-8, the final displacement variation on the FE-series theme. After relatively disappointing sales, the 7-Litre was demoted from full model line status to optional sport package in 1967. Few buyers noticed.

Ford's last shot at full-sized performance came in 1968 when Dearborn's better idea guys finally stuck GT badges on Galaxie fenders. Available only for big-block XLs, the optional GT equipment group helped distract buyers from the fact that sporty XL models no longer came with bucket seats and V-8 power as standard equipment. In 1969, the XL's sleek, new SportsRoof fastback body sweetened the GT pot considerably, as did the optional 360hp 429ci 385-series big-block V-8. Although the 429 would carry on, the '69 XL GT effectively ended Ford's big car performance bloodline.

Introduced in June 1962, the sporty XL package was created to help showcase Ford's hottest full-sized performance powerplants. Along with various exterior trim pieces, the top-line XLs featured front buckets, console and floor shifter, and an engine-turned dash insert. The '62 XL's factory-installed four-speed with floor shifter was a first for Ford; in 1961 an optional four-on-the-floor had debuted mid-year, but it was only available as a dealer-installed item.

Sitting two inches lower than its '62 forerunner, the '63-1/2 "fastback" Galaxie was a reported 28 percent more aerodynamic—a fact that instantly translated into major success on NASCAR's superspeedways. Recognizing that the "notchback" Galaxie profile was a veritable brick at high speeds, Ford's idea guys had tried to get away with attaching an optional "Starlift" roof to the '62 convertible to create a more swoopy shape for NASCAR competition. NASCAR rules moguls, however, didn't buy the idea, forcing Ford designers back to the drawing board. The result was this stylish, functional, mid-year bodystyle. To power the new fastback Galaxie, Ford engineers again beefed up the FE block, this time boring it out to 427ci—at least that's what they said. Actual displacement computed to 425ci, but Dearborn's image-makers apparently didn't want Ford's top performance powerplant to take a back seat to rival offerings. Seven liters, or roughly 427ci, was the established legal limit for stock-class racing, and with a flick of a public relations pen the new 425ci big-block was introduced to the public as being right at that limit. Triple carbs were dropped for 1963 in favor of two big Holley four-barrels. Counting both the single-carb 410hp and the dual-carb 425hp versions, Ford sold 4,978 427-equipped models in 1963.

Preceding pages
Undoubtedly the most prominent of the full-sized 427s was the '64 Galaxie. This was due largely to its overwhelming success on the 1964 NASCAR circuit where Ford garnered thirty wins, fifteen of those by Galaxie pilot Ned Jarrett. As in 1962 and 1963, Dearborn also built a special run of lightweight '64 Galaxies for A/Stock and B/Stock drag racing. Beneath a fiberglass, teardrop-scooped hood, A/Stock Galaxies were powered by a 427 High Riser, while the B/Stock cars used the "tamer" 427 Low Riser.

Identified only by two small front fender emblems, 427 Galaxies left many a streetside challenger wondering what hit him in 1964. All 427 Galaxies built in '63 and '64 were four-speed cars. Automatics were not available, though some '64 lightweight drag cars—like the Fairlane Thunderbolts—were fitted with Lincoln automatics. Equipped with 3.25:1 highway gears, a typical street-stock '64 427 Galaxie ran 0–60mph in 7.1sec and turned a 13.96sec quarter-mile during a *Speed & Custom* test.

Beneath that trademark oval air cleaner hide two 652cfm Holley four-barrel carburetors on an aluminum intake. Rated at 425hp, the dual-carb "R-code" 427 featured streamlined cast-iron headers, 11.5:1 compression, cross-bolted four-bolt main bearing caps, a solid-lifter cam, and chrome valve covers. Torque output was 480lb-ft at 3700rpm.

Performance-look accessories were of little concern to 427 Ford buyers in 1964, and additional gadgetry such as a tach and gauges weren't available. Not being a top-line XL model, this 427 Galaxie 500 features a somewhat spartan bench seat interior.

Wh(W)hat it is is lightning without thunder. It *moves*—but it moves like mist over a millpond, smoothly, quietly, effortlessly!

—Ford 7-Litre advertisement, 1965

Ads called the '66 7-Litre "either the quickest quiet car or the quietest quick car." Demonstrating that full-sized performance was already a thing of the past, the 1966 7-Litre was basically a sporty boulevard cruiser offering more luxury than performance. Standard equipment included front disc brakes and a 345hp 428ci engine. According to *Car Life*, a 345hp/C6 automatic 7-Litre could do no better than a 16.9sec ET in the quarter, a far cry from the 14sec runs clocked by '65 427 Galaxies. The optional 425hp 427 promised more bang for the buck, but reportedly only thirty-eight '66 7-Litres, including one convertible, were equipped with the king of the FEs.

Though it didn't make much difference, as the competition was doing it as well, the big Fords got bigger, gaining pounds and inches on a yearly basis.

—Phil Hall, *Fearsome Fords*

Along with this grille badge, standard 7-Litre exterior identification included similar emblems on the fenders and deck lid, body side striping, and mag-style wheel covers. The 7-Litre's die-cast aluminum grille is a standard Galaxie XL feature. Ford built 2,368 7-Litre convertibles for 1966; hardtop production was 8,705.

Left
Bucket seats, Ford's new Cruise-O-Matic C6 automatic transmission, a console with floor shifter, and a simulated wood-rimmed sport steering wheel were standard 7-Litre features. Optional equipment shown here includes a reclining passenger seat and the "Safety Convenience Control Panel," which houses five warning lights as a unit just above the console. Ford's top-loader four-speed manual was also available at extra cost, but apparently only 20 percent of 7-Litre buyers chose to do their own shifting.

A model series all its own in 1966, the 7-Litre was transformed into a mere options group in '67. Priced at $515.86, the "7-Litre Sport Package" again included the 345hp 428 backed by a C6 automatic, power front discs, and the bucket seat XL interior with a sport steering wheel. Although factory photos showed a twin-scooped hood and small, round fender emblems, most 7-Litres apparently carried no specific exterior identification save for the "428" fender badges. The familiar mag-style wheel covers were standard features in '66, but optional in '67. Approximately fifty 7-Litres were built in '67.

Opposite page
Essentially mechanically identical to the '66 7-Litre's standard 345hp 428, the '67 7-Litre powerplant featured chrome valve covers, which had been painted blue in 1966 like the open-element air cleaner. As in '66, the truly powerful 427 was a 7-Litre option in 1967.

This particular '67 7-Litre hardtop carries only one special piece of identification—this steering wheel hub medallion. Since any '67 Galaxie could have been ordered with a 428 V-8, the front fender badges did not necessarily denote the presence of a 7-Litre.

Left
Along with hideaway headlights, top-line XL models for 1969 received an exciting new "SportsRoof" shape featuring a recessed rear window. Combining the fresh XL face with the sporty GT equipment resulted in what Dearborn's advertising crew called "the Michigan strong boy." Ford's "sleek, solid, and silent" XL GT was also offered in convertible form. Popular options included a choice between a four-speed manual or SelectShift Cruise-O-Matic automatic, a limited-slip rearend, buckets seats, and a console.

In base form, a '69 XL GT was powered by a 265hp 390ci big-block V-8 topped by a two-barrel carburetor. Available at extra cost were two 429 big-blocks, one with a two-barrel (2V), the other with a four-barrel (4V). Output for the 429-2V was 320hp; the 429-4V made 360hp. In reference to the latter, Ford brochures claimed, "With 480 pounds of torque, this optional muscle machine could move a mountain"—a fair description considering the '69 XL GT weighed 4,135 pounds.

Chapter 4

Powered by Ford

Other Dearborn Developments

Although the 360hp 1960 Starliner may be considered Ford's first muscle car, Dearborn's performance tale actually began a few years earlier. A hot parts program had just gotten off the ground in 1957 when the infamous Automobile Manufacturers Association "ban" on factory racing shot it down. Early in the year, both Ford's regular passenger cars and its glamourous two-seat Thunderbirds had appeared with top performance versions of the 312ci Y-block V-8. Potent options included a dual-carb intake, radical cam kits, and a Paxton-built supercharger. But all that heavy-duty hardware quickly became museum pieces in February 1957 when the AMA moved to pull in the reins on Detroit's rapidly escalating horsepower race.

Another hot Thunderbird wouldn't appear until 1962, after Ford re-introduced the two-seat theme. With a special tonneau cover hiding its back seats, the Sports Roadster T-bird looked every bit the part of a per-formance machine. And with the optional "M-code" triple-carb 390ci V-8 beneath the hood, a Sports Roadster did feel mightier than the average 'Bird. Built in both 1962 and 1963, the M-code Thunderbird represented the last combination of personal luxury and performance.

Opposite page
A pair of Carroll Shelby's aces—the 289 Cobra (left) and its awesome 427ci variant. Featuring various competition modifications, this white small-block Cobra also wears FIA racing sheet metal—standard street versions of the 260 and 289 Cobras did not include the flaring needed to clear the wide racing rubber. Modifications required to fit the 427 in place of the 289 included a heavily reinforced chassis and coil springs at all four corners instead of the front and rear transverse leaf springs. The aluminum body's width grew seven inches thanks to the huge flares, and a more aggressive-looking snout with a larger grille opening was added to improve cooling.

To most minds, the '57 two-seat Thunderbird was a wonderfully classy personal luxury automobile, a vehicle perfect for a night on the town or a demonstration of status at the club. But a sports car it wasn't, although Ford initially offered two performance options to help put the thunder in Thunderbird. Known today by its serial number identification, the E-code '57 T-bird featured a 270hp 312ci Y-block V-8 with two four-barrel carburetors, while the F-code version replaced the two Holleys with a single Holley four-barrel force fed through a McCulloch centrifugal supercharger supplied by Paxton. Output for the blown 'Bird was 300hp, or 340hp with the optional NASCAR "racing kit."

While the Thunderbird was leaving performance behind, a former race driver from Texas was helping pick up the slack. Determined to build his own sports car after competing in others' for nearly ten years, Carroll Shelby had abandoned his racing career in 1960—thanks in part to a heart condition—and began seeking a new career as an automaker. In 1962, he combined a British sports car, the AC Ace, with Ford's new thin-wall-cast V-8, resulting in Shelby American's first AC Cobra, described by *Sports Car Graphic*'s editors as "one of the most impressive production sports cars we've ever driven." They spoke too soon. In 1963, Shelby replaced the 260ci V-8 with the enlarged 289ci version, then proceeded to squeeze every ounce of performance out of Dearborn's Windsor small-block. Race-ready 289 Cobras reportedly reached nearly 400hp, but even that wasn't enough.

In late 1964, Shelby unleashed his outrageous 427 Cobra. With huge Girling disc brakes at all four corners and 425 horses of FE-series big-block power beneath its aluminum skin, the 427 Cobra could rocket from rest to 100mph and back in 14.5sec. "That figure," reported *Car and Driver*, "is obtainable by the average Cobra driver with the regular 8.15x15 Goodyear Blue Dot street tires. [Shelby American racer] Ken Miles has done the job in as little as 13.8 seconds, and who knows how much improvement could be made with racing tires that would nullify some of the tremendous wheel spin?" There could be only one king of the American road in the sixties, and the 427 Cobra was it.

Along with helping create the 427 Cobra, Ken Miles had also assisted another British sport car builder with its Anglo-American hybrid. In April 1963, Miles had teamed with Britain's Rootes Motors to build a V-8-equipped Sunbeam Alpine prototype using Ford's 260ci small-block. Once refined, the Sunbeam Tiger emerged as what some considered the "poor man's Cobra." Later in December 1966, the 260 was replaced by a 200hp 289, with only 633 of the more powerful Mk II Tigers rolling off the Rootes line before production ceased in June 1967.

> I t was almost dangerous to put the Cobra in a showroom alongside your usual Detroit lead sled in 1964. The salesmen had to be properly educated just to demonstrate the car without killing themselves.
>
> —Wallace A. Wyss,
> *Shelby's Wildlife*

Two years before the Tiger's demise, Shelby American had introduced another Ford-powered street racer, this time using the Mustang as a base. Featuring a 306hp 289ci small-block, the GT350 was better suited to the track than the street, but subsequent renditions were gradually "civilized"—much to Shelby's dismay. In 1967, a second Shelby Mustang—the GT500 with its 428 big-block V-8—debuted to complement the 289-equipped GT350. The following year, Shelby Mustang production moved from Shelby American's Los Angeles facility to the A. O. Smith Company in Livonia, Michigan, with the last GT350s and 500s being built there in 1970.

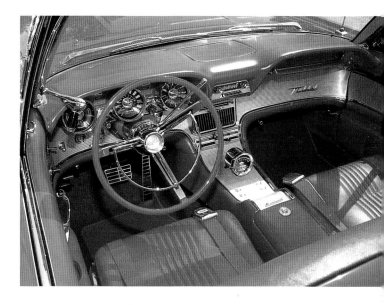

Aftermarket experiments with rear seat tonneau covers began appearing almost immediately after Ford had introduced the larger four-place Thunderbird in 1958. One of the more successful two-seat conversion efforts came from New Jersey Ford dealer Bill Booth, who also owned a fiberglass fabrication shop. Perhaps inspired by Booth's design, Ford stylist Bud Kaufman created a comparable cover that fit over the '62 Thunderbird's back seats and still allowed the convertible top to operate unheeded. Dearborn offered the Sports Roadster package as a factory option for '62; in '64 the attractive cover remained available as a dealer-installed feature.

Left
In 1962, Ford responded to requests for a return to the two-seat T-bird image by rolling out the Sports Roadster, a lavish showboat priced at a hefty $5,439. Included in the deal was a fiberglass tonneau cover with twin headrests that transformed the four-place 'Bird into a dream machine built for two. A dash-mounted grab bar for the passenger and four dazzling Kelsey-Hayes wire wheels completed the package. Sports Roadster production reached 1,427 in 1962; this '63 model is one of only 455 built. Bottom line for a '63 Sports Roadster was $5,563.

The grab bar on the passenger's side of the dash was included as part of the Sports Roadster package. Power steering and brakes, the three-speed Cruise-O-Matic automatic transmission, and the Swing-Away steering wheel were all standard Thunderbird features in 1963. With the transmission in park and the door open, the wheel would swing 10.5-inches to the left, allowing easy access. The wheel locked back in place once the transmission was shifted into drive.

To enhance the Sports Roadster's performance image, Ford engineers added a unique triple-carb intake to the Thunderbird's 390ci FE big-block V-8. Topped by three Holley two-barrels, the "M-code" aluminum manifold differed from the passenger car tri-carb setup due to the Thunderbird's "flat" engine position. A Galaxie V-8 slanted backward, meaning its intake was stair-stepped to keep the carburetors level; an M-code 390 manifold mounted all three carbs at the same height. Available for all Thunderbirds, the M-code 390 was rated at 340hp. Total

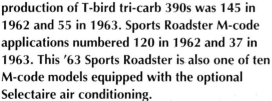

After seeing Carroll Shelby's success with his AC Cobra, officials from Great Britain's Rootes Group began plotting a similar Anglo-American hybrid in the spring of 1963. The resulting Sunbeam Tiger was priced around $3,500, weighed 2500lb, and initially featured a 164hp 260ci Ford small-block V-8. Reportedly, the car could go from rest to 100mph and back in less than 20sec. Regular production of Mk I Tigers began in June 1964. A slightly modified Mk IA was unveiled in August 1965, and the more powerful 289-powered Mk II rolled off the line in December 1966. Total production was 7,083. This '65 260 Tiger is one of 2,694 Mk IA models built.

production of T-bird tri-carb 390s was 145 in 1962 and 55 in 1963. Sports Roadster M-code applications numbered 120 in 1962 and 37 in 1963. This '63 Sports Roadster is also one of ten M-code models equipped with the optional Selectaire air conditioning.

With about seventy-five of his 260-powered AC Cobras built, Carroll Shelby made the switch to Ford's larger 289 Windsor small-block in 1963. Right out of the crate, the High Performance 289 was rated at 271hp. A few tweaks and some added compression bumped output even further and helped make the small-block Cobra a sizzling success. According to *Car Life*, a standard 289 Cobra with 3.77:1 gears managed 0–60mph in 5.7sec. Various potent options, such as these four Weber two-barrel carburetors, promised even quicker results.

Right
After Ken Miles had toyed with the idea of stuffing Ford's big 427 into the little Cobra, Shelby American began building big-block competition models in October 1964. Shelby's first completed 427 Cobra, CSX 3002, emerged in January 1965, beating CSX 3001 off the line while it waited for its completely restyled aluminum 427ci body shell. Additional 427 Cobra chassis modifications included widening the rear track 4.5-inches and front track 3.5-inches. From 1965 to 1967, Shelby American unleashed 348 427 Cobras in all-out racing, S/C (semi-competition), and street car forms.

Transforming a 2500lb British sports car into world-class road rocket was as simple as dropping 425hp worth of dual-carb 427ci Ford side-oiler V-8 beneath the bonnet. With 480lb-ft of torque, the 427 big-block transformed the already uncivilized Cobra into a downright savage. During a 1965 *Car and Driver* test, a 427 Cobra smoked the quarter-mile in 12.2sec at 118mph, easily the fastest time ever recorded by an American "production" vehicle.

Right

When first introduced in 1965, Shelby American's GT350 Mustang variant was a single-purpose machine available in one color only, without a back seat or an automatic transmission, and loaded with a full collection of standard race-ready hardware. In 1966, the car was tamed a bit as most of the hottest performance pieces became options and a back seat was added, along with various color choices and an optional C4 automatic. Big news for 1967 was an attractive make-over featuring various fiberglass components, an extended snout, and Cougar sequential taillights. This '67 GT350 lacks the popular dealer-installed Le Mans stripes, which ran parallel down the hood, roof, and deck lid.

Left
Shelby GT350 interior features included a Hurst shifter, a wood-rimmed sport steering wheel, an underdash gauge pod, an 8000rpm tachometer, and a 140mph speedometer. Shelby American built 1,175 small-block GT350s in 1967.

Heart of the GT350 from 1965 until 1967 was the Shelby-modified High Performance 289. Although the tri-Y headers used in '65 and '66 were exchanged for standard Ford cast-iron exhaust manifolds, advertised output for the "Cobra-ized" 289 remained at 306hp. Helping boost output from Ford's standard rating of 271hp was a 715cfm Holley four-barrel on an aluminum high-rise intake.

New for 1967 was a second Shelby Mustang model, the GT500, featuring a 428ci FE-series big-block V-8 as standard equipment. Featuring two 600cfm Holley four-barrels on an aluminum intake, the Shelby 428 was rated at 355hp. Both the GT500 and GT350 received the same styling upgrades, including a fiberglass nose that added three inches to total length. The fiberglass hood with its functional scoop, the lower valance panel, and the grille were all unique '67 Shelby features, as were the twin 7in driving lights. Since some states specified a minimum distance between headlights, many Shelby Mustangs have these lights mounted apart at each end of the grille.

New '67 Shelby bodywork in back included brake-cooling scoops, rear-quarter ventilators, and a duck-tail deck lid with matching rear-quarter spoiler ends, all made of fiberglass. Notice the optional Le Mans stripes. The 15in Mag Star aluminum center/steel rim wheels were also optional. This '67 GT500 is one of 2,050 built. Thanks to the big-block GT500's introduction, Shelby Mustang sales jumped 35 percent for 1967.

Right
Although not officially offered as a Shelby American option in '67, Ford's 425hp 427ci side-oiler V-8 did find its way into a few '67 GT500s. With only half of Shelby American's factory invoices for 1967 presently available, another two 427 GT500s have been documented. But since any dealer could have made the swap on request and an owner could have requested the change at additional cost if he blew his 428 under warranty, there's no telling how many 427 '67 Shelbys hit the streets. Non-stock items on this 427 include a Mallory distributor and aftermarket headers.

Index